REFRESHING

Rekindle Your Passion For Life!

GINA C. EDWARDS

Refreshing: Rekindle Your Passion For Life! Copyright © September 2020

By Gina C. Edwards

Published in the United States of America by

ChosenButterflyPublishing LLC

www.cb-publishing.com

Scriptures marked KJV are taken from the KING JAMES VERSION (KJV): KING JAMES VERSION, public domain.

Scripture quotations marked (TLB) are taken from The Living Bible copyright © 1971. Used by permission of Tyndale House Publishers, a Division of Tyndale House Ministries, Carol Stream, Illinois 60188. All rights reserved.

Scriptures marked AMP are taken from the AMPLIFIED BIBLE (AMP): Scripture taken from the AMPLIFIED® BIBLE, Copyright © 1954, 1958, 1962, 1964, 1965, 1987 by the Lockman Foundation Used by Permission. (www.Lockman.org)

Scripture quotations marked (NLT) are taken from the Holy Bible, New Living Translation, copyright © 1996, 2004, 2007, 2013, 2015 by Tyndale House Foundation. Used by permission of Tyndale House Publishers, Inc., Carol Stream, Illinois 60188. All rights reserved.

Scripture marked (The Voice) are taken from The Voice™. Copyright © 2012 by Ecclesia Bible Society. Used by permission. All rights reserved.

Scriptures marked (MGG) have been taken from The Message Bible. Copyright Â© 1993, 1994, 1995, 1996, 2000, 2001, 2002. Used by permission of NavPress Publishing Group."

All rights reserved under International Copyright Law. Contents and/or cover may not be reproduced, distributed, or transmitted in any form or by any means or stored in a database or retrieval system, without the prior written consent of the publisher and/or authors.

ISBN: 978-1-945377-14-3

First Edition Printing

Printed in the United States of America

September 2020

Acknowledgements and Dedication

Thank you to everyone who supported me as I journeyed through this book. Thank you, Lisa Frazier, for your assistance and to my Pastors Anthony and Glenda Bailey, for writing the foreword. Thank you to Apostle Anita Hopes and Anthony "Chip" Bailey for your book testimonies.

This book is dedicated to my wonderful mother, Mrs. G. Marie Edwards.
You always have a glow of love upon you!
Thank you for your continual strength and refreshment in my life.

~Gina

Book Endorsements

Thank you Gina for writing this inspiring book about faith and how to accomplish our dreams. You not only showed us the necessity of it, but gave us the fundamental and practical steps to assure our success. I loved the part where you admonished us to take time, be still, and observe God's handiwork in nature. In these times we hear most clearly.

May the work of your hands continue to prosper!

~*Apostle Anita Hopes*

"Empowering! Encouraging! Refreshing! This book is right on time, giving you practical, Bible-based instruction that can be applied to your life TODAY! As a creative, I've encountered many rejections that made me second guess my God-given creativity. But then I read a passage that resonated with my spirit - *"Creativity sparks your faith to extend beyond your confined boundaries, to extend beyond your abilities and to trust in God's super-abilities."*

I was reminded that my creativity comes from God and when His hand is on it, it will prosper. Knowing that alone gave me all the confidence in the world. I assure you after reading this book, you will be empowered, encouraged and *Refreshed*!"

Thank you for this book Min. Gina!

God bless you!

~Anthony "Chip" Bailey

Contents

Acknowledgements and Dedication

Book Endorsements

Foreword

Introduction 1

Refresh Your Life by:

1. Finding a Time of Rest 7
2. Rekindling Your Purpose 11
3. Utilizing Your Creativity 19
4. Regenerating the Newness of Life 27
5. Exercising Gratefulness and Grace 37
6. Experiencing God's Presence 43
7. Declaring God's Strength 51
8. Recovering Your Peace 57
9. Walking Out Your Faith 63
10. Understanding the Vision 69

11. Creating an Atmosphere of Worship 75

12. Remembering Who You Are 81

Conclusion 89

Time of Application 91

Other Books by Gina C. Edwards 94

Biography 95

Foreword

There is nothing like being in a desert place in your life – a dry place where it seems like you are defeated – not able to have a win in your life. You are saved and sanctified – believe in, trust in, walk in, and sleep in the Word of God. You work hard, take care of your responsibilities, pay your bills, mind your own business, and don't bother anybody. Yet, you still trust God. You could also be dealing with an illness for a short or long period of time, having to stand in faith and believe God for your healing. We would submit to you that you need a "Refreshing" from God.

When we started reading this book, we immediately felt the 'Refreshing' from God that we so needed. It was like pouring cold water over our heads in the dead heat of a hot summer day. This book will remind you of what God said in His Word about renewing your mind. Dreams and visions were awakened again that had been drained out of us from the day-to-day rigors of life. Moreover, the break and renewal that we would usually get from a conference, we received in this book. Don't get us wrong, we never lost our hope or trust in God. But in our continually working (while tired and drained) and refreshing others, we tend to put ourselves on the back burner while needing to be refreshed. We were reminded and renewed in our purpose for life. All we can say is "But God." His grace kept and sustained us.

Like us, we're sure you can identify with one if not several of life's issues. However, there are tools that God has given to the Body of Christ to help us navigate this thing called "life". This book is one of those tools. It presents scriptural, line-upon-line, and precept-upon-precept principles and encouragement that will stir your soul and spirit to complete the assignment God has on your life. It is full of nuggets that will inspire you for the rest of your life. Receive your own Refreshing as you read this book.

Gina – We are so godly proud of you and your obedience to what He has entrusted you with. Know that He has much more in store for you. Pay no attention to the distractions. They are insignificant when compared to your purpose. We love you, we support you, and are again so godly proud of you.

A Servant's Heart,
Pastors Anthony and Glenda Bailey
Word Alive Worship Center

Introduction

In December 2019, I was seeking God about my next book title and I kept hearing in my spirit the word—Refreshing, Refreshing, Refreshing! I thought it was an invigorating, breathtaking and inviting title, so relevant for today's believer. Balancing work, family, dreams and ministry can take a toll on you if you don't take time for reflection, self-care and a respite. This book is a message of restoration for the Body of Christ.

Sometimes during your spiritual journey, you may face a quandary: Is my walk with Christ developing and growing as needed? Will I fulfill the calling on my life in my lifetime or am I seeking God for a new beginning or a personal revival?

Do you happen to need a refreshing? If so, you are not alone. We all do: Moms, Dads, Pastors, College Students, Retirees, Wives and Husbands. As diverse as we are with unique needs and experiences, the one thing we have in common is that we all need a fresh breath of life at times. Let's first understand the word Refresh, according to the Merriam/Webster Dictionary:

Refresh is defined as "to restore strength, to freshen up, to update or renew."

If you have ever been joyless, stagnant, unproductive, unfulfilled, or maybe your desire to serve has even decreased with time, you can be encouraged today because to refresh means to reactivate something already present. You don't have to find it! You don't have to look for it! Your gifting, your power, your strength already dwells within you, through the power of Jesus Christ.

I admit the daily duties of life can be mundane! At times I've been so busy with work, church, adjunct teaching, serving on non-profit boards and family that I didn't have the time or energy to be creative or enjoy the fruits of life. Many times, I felt empty, unfulfilled and knew it was time for a change! It was time for a refreshing in my life!

This is the day the Lord has made, I will rejoice (I will choose to rejoice) and be glad in it. (Psalm 118:24). Life is about choices! Good choices, bad choices, delayed choices and even emotional choices. How we interact with life and our circumstances is all centered on choices. Part of living a refreshed life is choosing a new outlook each day. You could wake up feeling frustrated, unmotivated, discouraged or you could wake up excited and thankful for a new start in life.

Did you know your choices can determine whether or not you walk in a time of refreshment? You can let life rob you of each daily blessing God has bestowed upon you or you can embrace life and enjoy it with gratefulness. It doesn't mean you walk on a bed of roses but you do find the good and grace of each day. Believe me, I understand that we face some challenging situations; death, layoffs, disappointments, divorce, miscarriages, and diseases, to name a few. How do you walk refreshed when you are still dealing with the circumstances of life? You first recognize that life is a journey. Where you are today is not your final destination. Every step of your life is woven together in a beautiful masterpiece. Next, you exercise the principles of God's Word through faith, which requires your participation.

From this book you will be reminded that you matter to God! There is beauty in knowing that God hears your prayers and is concerned about the things that concern you. For that we give Him praise! What a refreshing perspective to embrace! The Master of the universe thinks about you every day. You will further be reminded that our source of life is from God and we are to daily draw from His endless pool of strength and grace. This book will empower you to take a deep breath, spread your wings and activate the ingenuity that dwells in you.

To further comprehend refreshment, let's look at it from a natural perspective:

- After sitting in the hot sun all day on the beach, the wind begins to stir and a burst of air caresses your face.
- You've pressed through the mile charity walk and finally

- come to the finish line. An ice-cold bottle of water awaits you. You brush the bottle against your forehead before engulfing its soothing and cool contents.
- You get into your hot car out of the 100-degree weather and turn on the air conditioner full blast. Your skin cools down as sweat dries from your face.

These natural methods of refreshing are inviting, but they do not outweigh the spiritual refreshing we desperately need. Just like we welcome an external refreshment, we need an internal renewing as well. The rivers of living water flow through you, my friend. Therefore, you have access to a refreshing every day, at any time. Yes, the spark of life still lives in you! You have the ability not just to capture life but to accomplish your dream with confidence, bringing them both to fruition. In this new time of enlightenment, life is beginning anew. Are you ready for a refreshing?

Isaiah 61:3 states, *"To console those who mourn in Zion, to give them beauty for ashes, the oil of joy for mourning. The garment of praise for the spirit of heaviness; that they may be called tress of righteousness, the planting of the Lord, that He may be glorified."* This scripture is referring to the children of God who are living in pain, disappointment, discouragement and who have been overwhelmed by the toils of life. Isaiah encouraged the people that God would give them beauty for ashes, the oil of joy for mourning and the garment of praise for the spirit of heaviness. My sister and brother, I declare joy, hope, restoration and gladness back into your life or maybe you just need a reminder that you were created for greatness!

As you read through this book, ask God to ignite some broken dreams, heal some broken promises and rejuvenate broken hope. This is your time to embrace balance, receive clarity of thought and digest the contents of each chapter. This is your time to receive your personal refreshing. It is awaiting you today and every day!

"The law of the Lord is perfect (flawless), Restoring and refreshing the soul!"

(Psalm 19:7)

REFRESHING

Chapter 1

Refresh Your Life by Finding a Time of Rest

It seems like the weekends go by so fast. You are ripping and running around completing all of your errands and finishing chores at home. You could be raising a family, growing your career or working in ministry. Before you know it, you are back to work on Monday morning and you are already tired. When we get bogged down with the responsibilities of home life, work, church and extracurricular activities, the dream that was fervent seems to die and the spice for life dwindles. We even find that our outlook on life can become stale or stagnant. We get caught between the desire to do more and "I don't have time to do another thing." We look back over our lives and don't see the goals that we've planned actualized. We don't see the progress we had expected and wonder if we will ever achieve that dream or accomplishment.

After a while, the exciting goals and dreams drift into the back of our thoughts, becoming more of a memory than a reality. How do you break free from this draining cycle? What you need to do is carve out time to rest and to be spiritually energized so your heart and mind are renewed, bringing forth healing, peace and even the ability to dream again.

One of my greatest challenges in finding rest is quieting my thoughts and turning my brain off from all that I've done that day and still need to do that week. So it's imperative for me to have down time before going to bed, even if I have to just listen to music or sit peacefully for a minute. I know this is easier said than done. Yet a time of rest and renewal is important for the following reasons:

- Rest relieves stress, the physical, chemical, or emotional factor that causes bodily or mental tension.
- Rest gives your body time to heal and rejuvenate.
- Rest allows you to tune into God's frequency.
- Rest opens the door to creativity and strategic planning. If your mind is in overload it is hard to expand your thinking beyond what is absolutely necessary.
- Rest gives you strength to enjoy the benefits of life.

When you take time to rest (physically and spiritually), your spirit and mind are recharged. You can rest knowing that God is your daily bread; He is your lifeline! Psalm 73:25 & 26 says it so well: *"Whom have I in Heaven but you? And there is none upon earth that I desire besides You. My flesh and my heart fail; But God is the strength of my heart and my portion forever."* When you trust God, you relieve yourself of the cares of life.

God desires that we come to Him. Your relationship with Him allows you to live and breathe and have your being in our creator God. We exist only because He exists. God fills us, sustains us, and revives our souls. Our lives are completely interlocked with Him. When you draw near to God, His only response will be to draw near to you.

Draw means "to cause to move continuously towards." You are to continually seek God and pursue Him. You will not be disappointed! Father God loves when you seek Him over everything else. He loves to be with you and share with you. Jeremiah 33:3 reads, *"Call to me and I will answer you and show you great and mighty (inaccessible) things which you do not know."* How empowering to know God will share with you hidden treasures; treasures of Heaven, treasures of His character and even treasures of your future.

As you thirst for more of God, your heart will overflow with rivers of living water, which is the Spirit of the living God. Water represents life (spiritually and naturally). Let the Spirit of God wash away your past, your hurts, and your insecurities. You do this by washing your heart and mind with the Word of God. The Word renews your mind and cleanses it from old, negative thinking.

Furthermore, we need an outpouring of God's Spirit in our hearts and over our land. In the Bible water represents the Holy Spirit; He operates just like water. He refreshes, restores, and renews you. Even as water gives life, refreshing the earth, so does the Holy Spirit give life to your being—body, soul and mind!

God wants you to operate in rest and restoration. This is shared in Jeremiah 31:25 (The Message Bible): *"I'll refresh tired bodies; I'll restore tired souls."* I'm a candidate for this, how about you? Ask the Holy Spirit for a renewal in your physical body and in your spiritual walk. Then release your day to God each evening so you can rest in peace that night. Proverbs 3:24 reminds us that, *"When you lie down, you will not be afraid; Yes, you will lie down and your sleep will be sweet."* When you have received sweet rest, you will be able to support your family, sow into others, and serve with greater power!

> *"And He said, "My Presence will go with you,*
> *And I will give you rest."*
>
> **(Exodus 33:14)**

Chapter 2

Refresh Your Life by Rekindling Your Purpose

God is the ultimate planner and scheduler. He is able to orchestrate all things for your good and purpose. What is purpose? It is something set up as an object or end to be attained. Are you where you think you should be in your life right now? Have you reached your objective end for some of your goals? Even if you haven't accomplished everything on your bucket list yet, God has you aligned in the right position for that open door, for that unexpected call or for that divine connection. His omniscience knows every step of your journey. Therefore, nothing surprises Him. Good news! Where you are right now does not alarm God. You are right on schedule. But sometimes we all need a little stirring to move us in the right direction.

In 2 Timothy 1:6–7, Paul admonished Timothy (his spiritual son) about the work of the ministry. He encouraged him to stir up the gift within him. Stir means "to feel a strong emotion and a desire to do something." A synonym of the word "stir" is the word "passion," which is defined as "a strong liking or desire for or devotion to some activity, object or concept."

What are you passionate about?

- Your sweetheart
- A favorite sports team
- Your advancing career
- Obtaining more education
- Fulfilling a dream

Whatever it is you must have this same devotion to fulfill your purpose. If you do not possess this drive, who else will?

The word "stir" in Greek is "anazopureo," meaning to kindle afresh or rekindle. This means the fire missing from your life is still in the depths of your soul! It might be dormant but you haven't lost anazopureo. Your gift, your dream, your purpose still has life! This reminds me of the season of springtime. During the winter, all of the leaves fall off the trees and plants; nature seems dull and lifeless. Nevertheless, there is still the sap of life in each branch, twig and tree. When spring manifests, buds begin to sprout into flowers and leaves until they are in full bloom. The unfolding of life appears right before your eyes. Soon, plants, trees and flowers are flourishing, arraying the earth with their beauty; fulfilling their purpose for another season.

Let's examine the word "gift". A gift is a natural ability or talent like that of an athlete, musician, poet or chef. Now, a spiritual gift is a divine empowerment, an anointing given to each believer, graced by the Holy Spirit, to accomplish a specific ministry for the body of Christ, examples include giving, leading, faith, and encouraging. Is your gift on fire? Is it stirred up?

Two thousand and eight was an impactful year for me. Let me share how some of my gifts were stirred. After presenting a play I co-wrote at my church, Word Alive Worship Center, a prophetic word came forth from my pastor that empowered me. I was tired of being unfulfilled, over and over again. Therefore, I committed to launching out into the unknown. I immediately begin writing a full musical play, script and songs. I sought God for direction, researched my craft and started, little by little, putting my dream into action. I even planned dates of the play to force myself to commit to this project. More importantly, I could envision the whole play. I mean I saw every scene unfold in my spirit. What was birthed, in 2009, was a musical gospel play called *Seasons of Life* with a cast of 13 and stage crew of four.

This faith experience taught me several things:
- I had to take action with my dream. No one else was going to do it for me.
- I was not waiting on God; He was waiting on me to activate my faith. This was an awakening moment.

- Unbelief and inaction will steal your time.

Therefore, I empower you to understand your gift, grow it, and then guard your gift. I'll speak more about identifying and growing your gift in Chapter 10; however, I will address now why you need to guard your gift. God has anointed each of us with gifts to equip and edify the church (Ephesians 4:11 & 12). The enemy will send every obstacle and distraction to take you off your course. I've learned that when you are preparing to step out on faith or fulfill a destiny purpose, you receive much warfare. In the warfare you can get so frustrated that you throw your gift away, put it on a shelf or misuse it. That's why it is imperative to have accountability partners to keep you focused, keeping your eyes on the prize. Therefore, you must protect the anointing that God has given you. It will be used to set others free and ignite faith in them.

God knows the plans He has for you but it's not always obvious. Sometimes your purpose is hidden in unconventional and uncomfortable situations. When your back is against a wall, somehow an unused or dormant gift springs forth into action, surprising everyone including you. I love when God unfolds another layer of purpose before your eyes; something you never expected to happen to you.

Your purpose is not stifled or constrained by your past, what you see or understand. God works outside of natural boundaries. He has no limit, therefore you do not! Your future is filled with greatness! So don't constrain your hopes. *"Eye has not seen, nor ear heard, nor have entered into the heart of mankind, the things which*

God has prepared for those who love Him" (1 Corinthians 2:9). You were created and prewired to succeed! That's right—the only option is up!

You can't afford to get easily distracted by things that don't have eternal merit; a relationship that didn't work out, someone doesn't like you or if you are wearing the latest fashions. These things waste time, drain your energy and emotions and are temporary. If you could focus (give direct attention) each day on the eternal beauty of life and how it impacts others, you would be much happier.

God wants you to know that He has already gone before you in your journey and that He has prepared the way for you. He can accomplish this because He already knows what your future holds. He sees the end before the beginning and then gives you a glimpse into your future. It's called dreaming. Amazing!

What if your purpose was a casualty of unforeseen circumstances? If your purpose was broken because of pain in your life, it can be healed again; whether that is from broken relationships, broken dreams, broken promises or financial woes. God is a purpose healer and He makes all things new (Colossians 3:10). Nothing is outside of His wheelhouse or expertise. There is never a situation that is so dire that God cannot revive it. You just need to apply a word of faith on it, a rhema word.

A rhema word always rekindles your purpose. Rhema is a Greek word meaning "a specific word or utterance from the Lord that quickens your soul." Have you ever heard a sermon, listened to a song or read a scripture that spoke to your current situation? I mean it touched the depths of your soul and sparked a light inside of you. This rhema word propelled you to believe again and to pursue purpose again. You know that word was meant just for you. Now that describes a rhema word! We need God's prophetic work and quickening as we walk out our purpose and uncover the treasures that He has for us. A treasure is something valuable, important or special that is hidden or kept in a safe place. Do you know what God is unveiling to you in this season? I guarantee you, whatever that may be, it is not just for you.

The Bible encourages us to comfort others as we are comforted. In like manner, we are to refresh others as we have been refreshed. This is accomplished as you understand and fulfill your purpose; then you should impact other people's lives in a greater manner. I call this concept "imparting eternity," which was the title of my first book. This is the ability to sow into other people an eternal moment, a moment that can never be taken away from them. It could be an encouraging word that changes that person's destiny, the prayer of salvation or a song that brings healing.

Jeremiah 29:11 confirms that God has given each of us a purpose; a purpose filled with peace and hope. He is confident that our future is bright! Embrace your purpose with boldness and determination, for there is no one else who can fulfill your purpose but you! No one else can contribute to the earth what you can. No one else can reach the souls that you are assigned to. I declare that your purpose has been reborn and rekindled to life again!

"And we know (with great confidence) that God (who is deeply concerned about us) causes all things to work together (as a plan) for good for those who love God, to those who are called according to His plan and purpose."

(Romans 8:28, Amplified)

REFRESHING

Chapter 3

Refresh Your Life by Utilizing Your Creativity

A rt is something that is created with imagination and precision. It comes in many variations like music, paintings or sculptures and it represents a diverse culture, in addition to emerging ideas or feelings. Art is birthed with intention and purpose! Like art, you are created with purpose, incredible value and beauty! You are a masterpiece, unique in so many ways. Ephesians 2:10 describes the believer as God's craftsmanship or workmanship: "the quality imparted to a thing in the process of making." You are wonderfully complex, intricately and perfectly created in the image of God. He breathed His life and creative nature into you. In Genesis 1, God said, "Let there be," and it was! Your words are that powerful as well and can shape the world you abide in.

When you think of God's handiwork and the specific time He took to make and create the world, it's absolutely marvelous! If you ever had the of privilege of gazing on the beauty of places like Yellowstone redwood trees, the Northern Lights, Niagara Falls, the clear waters of the Bahamas or the jaw-dropping Grand Canyon, you would quickly recognize that these earthly wonders did not appear on their own accord. Someone greater than the elements of nature had to be creatively at work.

Can you imagine this same creative power and ingenuity lives in you? When you think of the intellect of mankind and the technological advancements we have made throughout history, it's not surprising to see space travel, auto-driven cars, and artificial intelligence. Whoever thought that cars could drive themselves? Has the *Jetsons* cartoon become a reality? God wants you to exemplify Philippians 4:13 to the world. *I can do all things through Christ who strengthens me.* As you do this you reveal His glory in the earth and make God's name known.

Let's look at the word "creativity," it means "to have the ability to create or transcend traditional ideas or use your imagination." What have you created with the gifts God has given you? Do you happen to feel stuck?

If you do, it is time for you to take a leap of faith or, as I call it, Casting the Net. In John 21:1–6, after Christ's resurrection, the disciples went back to their earthly vocation. They were disappointed and had lost hope. So they went back to the familiar, they went fishing. One evening, the experienced fishermen fished all night long and were unsuccessful. When morning came, Christ was observing their situation from the beach and told them to cast their net to the right side, to the other side of the boat. In spite of their losing streak, they conceded to obey His command and caught more fish than they could manage. We know that the fish represented souls albeit the disciples didn't realize that at the time.

However, this passage of scripture also reveals that sometimes you just have to try again. You have to go into the deep and not stay in the shallow, safe waters. We tend to give up too quickly in our pursuit of our goals and dreams. Sometimes we are so stuck in our ways and comfortable in our fears that we do not take the leap of faith into the unknown. Be determined to cast your net into a greater tomorrow! Be determined to mandate more from your life. Be determined to expect more every day!

Our faith is tested when we step out of the familiar, when we grow in our gifting or follow our dreams. In faith you face situations greater than yourself. This is where your gifts are stretched and you experience conflict that can't be figured out in the natural. Believe it or not, this is by design! You only grow when you are challenged, feel out of your league, or step out of comfortability. Only then are you forced to rely on God; otherwise you will remain in your present stage, stagnant and stale. Dare to believe that your latter days are greater than your past.

Creativity sparks your faith to extend beyond your confined boundaries, to extend beyond your abilities and to trust in God's super-abilities. In fact, God challenges us with the words of this scripture: *"Now to Him who is able to do exceeding, abundantly above all that we ask of think, according to the power that works in us"* (Ephesians 3:20). God can go beyond your extended imagination and your astounding dreams. The question is do you have the faith to imagine more than you can see with your naked eye? Who says you can't be a millionaire? Who says you can't write a television show or movie? Who says you won't be on the cover of *Forbes*? My friend, I believe you haven't dreamed or lived out your greatest achievement in life yet. Wow!

Therefore, you must foster or nurture your creative side. Do you know when you are most creative or when you have the greatest ideas? I find I am most creative in the morning time. This is when I do my best writing. There are no disturbances, just peace and quiet to flow with God's thoughts. Other things that spark my creativity include the grandeur of nature or even a song. I've learned that everything I do (writing of a song, a book or a message) is all inspired by God. In other words, I can't say, "That was a good idea," without giving God the glory. *"Every good thing given and every perfect gift (idea or innovation) is from above; it comes down from the Father of lights (the Creator and Sustainer of the Heavens) above"* (Paraphrased from James 1:17, Amplified).

Something else that energizes my imagination is watching *Shark Tank*. How about you? This show displays the power of inventiveness and entrepreneurship. Every time I watch the show it reminds me that you can achieve your dreams if you persevere and believe in yourself. God has given each of us the power to get wealth. He has given us the ability to have multiple streams of income and walk in financial breakthrough. Have you found your avenue of wealth yet? Ask God for wisdom, sow into the Kingdom, apply His Word into your heart, then prepare and plan for it. The right opportunities will manifest!

Spontaneity is an undetermined action or movement. I believe as adults we have forgotten how to have fun and how to do things that are NOT planned. When was the last time you played a board game or charades or did something unscheduled? Technology has its place but it seems to have stolen the ability to have fun or relate to others. We now have less face time and less family dinners because we are engrossed in our tablets or game applications. Spontaneity breeds creativity!

What are you doing to revive your daily routine? I challenge you to go ahead and have some fun. Go somewhere new, go to a concert out of state or stay in a hotel for the weekend. Take your spouse on a date night or go to dinner with some friends. When was the last time you laughed so hard you began crying? Laughter is good for the soul! Mayo Clinic (a non-profit organization that is dedicated to whole-person care) shares the benefits of laughter as the ability to:

- Relieve stress and even pain.
- Improve your immune system with positive thoughts.
- Enhance your oxygen intake, which stimulates your organs.

We all need these benefits! Amen!

One of the greatest ways I enjoy laughter and capture spontaneity is through my grandson-—Caleb. Grandchildren are so refreshing and special! And if you don't have any grandchildren, spend time with your nieces or nephews or your Godchildren. They brighten up your day, make you grin from ear to ear and lead you into silly activities that evoke contagious laughter. I love when my grandson and I see each other. We meet with great joy and excitement beaming from our eyes.

How refreshing it is to engage with grandchildren in the most simplistic childhood games, like hide and go seek, building forts or play fighting with superheroes. My grandson says, "I'm happy! Are you happy, Gigi?"

"Yes I am, Caleb," I respond.

Anything that went wrong that day dissolves in seconds and reminds me of what's truly important in life. Grandchildren give you a new perspective on life. Things aren't as serious as they appear when you look at them through the lens of a child.

Grandchildren are an extension of you and represent your legacy. Therefore, you must ensure that your legacy is covered in prayer. You constantly pray for their peace and protection. You declare that they are marked for the Kingdom of God and that only God's purpose will be performed in their lives. They are different than your own children because you're not responsible for their day-to-day care. When you see them, it's for pure enjoyment! Find time to spring laughter into your soul again.

Tap into your life source and expand your possibilities!

Refresh your creativity and spark an undetermined action; try writing a song or poem, develop a new online business, or sign up for a class for fun. God desires to partner with you to bring forth His incredible and perfect plan in the earth. The possibilities of new beginnings are truly endless! Ask God to reveal one to you tonight!

"A gift does wonders; it will bring you before men of importance!"
(Proverbs 18:16, TLB)

REFRESHING

Chapter 4

Refresh Your Life by Regenerating the Newness of Life

I love to hear the birds singing in the morning. I imagine each song calls forth the announcement of a new day, a new adventure and new sights to discover. What a pleasant and calming way to start your day! It's a joyful reminder of the newness of life. What needs to be renewed in you? How about changing an old habit, increasing your prayer time or adopting a positive mindset? Some old habits have been with you for years and all of the wishing will not alleviate them. It takes more than willpower to release an old habit; you need dedication, accountability and action to see change. How is your prayer life? Prayer is not just meant for church or for gracing your food. Prayer is a continual communication with God. It is a time to give God glory, convey your gratefulness and intercede for others. Equally important, prayer is a time to be quiet and listen to the heart of God.

Do you have any old mindsets that are holding you back?

- I'm not good enough
- I would pursue my dream if I wasn't afraid
- I will never meet my true love
- My father was never in my life so why bother?
- I wish I could change my past

These old mindsets need to be replaced with promises from the Bible. God's Word produces life and fruit; He promised that it won't return to Him empty. But it must be exercised through confession, by faith, on a daily basis. Here are a few precious promises to meditate on:

- *"Call to Me, and I will answer you, and show you great and mighty things, which you do not know."* (Jeremiah 33:3)
- *"And let us not grow weary while doing good, for in due season we shall reap if we do not lose heart."* (Galatians 6:9)
- *"The Lord is good to those who wait for Him, To the soul who seeks Him."* (Lamentations 3:25)

Doesn't that make you feel better already? God's Word elevates your spirit. God's Word even penetrates the impoverished soul. The enemy is a skillful and manipulator of words and will tell you lies, false truths and half-truths about yourself or your situation. He is the facilitator of taking the sins of your past and present to weigh you down. Yes, sin is a heavy burden, but you don't have to bear it. Jesus specifically died to take away the penalty, punishment and power of sin in your life. Confess it and move forward (1 John 1:9). Therefore, you can't wallow in it! The enemy will condemn you so don't condemn yourself. Remember he is the accuser of each one of us. However, through the resurrection of Jesus, God will redeem, revive and refresh your soul! He who the Son sets free is free indeed.

1 Corinthians 5:17 states, *"Therefore, if anyone is in Christ he or she is a new creation; old things have passed away; behold all things are new."* New is defined as "being other than the former or old." Our spirit man is made anew when we are born again. Hallelujah! God demonstrates to us the newness of life in His daily mercy, in His manifested love and in every second a baby is born; new miracles unfold. God's spirit in us transforms our thoughts, ideas and behavior as we journey through this unique pattern of life. With time your perspective begins to change and old thoughts are replaced with God's Word.

Let me explain transformation this way. If you are in the mountains looking down into the valley, you can see the city from a broader perspective. At this level you observe, from on high, the buildings, the trees, the streets and the schools and how the blocks align together. However, when you are walking around in the city, your vision is limited; you can only see what's before you. It's important to change our perspective and see things the way God (the Lord Most High) sees them. He continually manifests unknown things to you. Even though you may not understand it now, be assured that God knows how to reveal Himself to you. God knows how to reach you.

God personifies new beginnings through creation, through salvation and even through a smile. Every day is a new day to start all over again. *"But one thing I do, forgetting those things which are behind and reaching forward to those things which are ahead."* (Philippians 3:13). Nature demonstrates this concept so effortlessly. Spring is not bound by the harsh winter. It bursts forth boldly onto the scene, demanding the stage. Flowers blossom; birds sing; the temperature gets warmer, inviting a season of hope!

Consequently, release those things that are behind you; the disappointments, the broken promises and even your own failures. Accept the realization that you are not perfect but you are complete in God. This was a rhema word for me. So often we think that because we have problems or life issues, God can't use us. As you come to Him with a humble heart, God finds ways to use your imperfections for His glory! Yes, you are still going to make mistakes, but you have to learn from such moments so they are not repeated. God has high expectations for you and desires that you succeed in this one life that you have. And He has equipped you to fulfill this earthly mission. Would you dare to believe again? Let's make a commitment to focus forward!

Life is a gift! We must live each day maximizing its opportunities, exploring God's wonders and extending ourselves to one another. The appreciation of life really impacted me when I heard about the untimely deaths of Myles Munroe, Kobe Bryant and even my late father. They were great in their own ways; nevertheless, they left this earth earlier than we desired. Uneventful moments like these make you stop, pause and reflect on your own life journey. *Am I doing absolutely everything I'm supposed to be doing with this limited time I have on earth? Am I allowing fear, worry or my past to hinder me?*

It's time to enjoy the adventures of this faith walk. It doesn't mean you have to be rich or famous to enjoy life, but I encourage you to find a way to maximize each day. How can you be an extension of God's hand and His heart? Think of ways you can be used to walk in the ministry of reconciliation. It's so empowering and refreshing when the eyes of your heart are finally enlightened to your daily purpose.

Moreover, I realize that every day is filled with experiences and opportunities not just to live for ourselves but to better mankind. I understood why purpose must be fulfilled and not toiled with because of a tethered past. Listen to this encounter I experienced: I visited a local convenience store one Sunday afternoon to get lunch for my mother. There was a man standing outside the door asking for money. On my way out of the store, he asked me for change and I told him I didn't have any, which was true. But boy did I feel guilty for not doing something for him. I proceeded home with my purchases, but my spirit was not at rest. A mile later, I made a U-turn, returned to the store and bought him something to eat. What's the purpose of sharing this experience? To remind you that if you have the ability and power to bring sunshine into someone's life—just do it! I couldn't afford not to help him. You never know how your life will bless someone if you just extend yourself beyond your own conveniences.

Today is a new opportunity to revive your commitment to God! It's time to return to your first love if you have drifted away:

- Remember why you received salvation in the first place.
- Restart your quiet time with God. He desires to commune with you.
- Expand from reading one verse a day to one chapter of the Bible a day. Ask the Holy Spirit to reveal His Word to you.
- Communicate with God throughout the day and expect to hear back from Him.

Yes, it's time for a fresh pouring out of the Holy Spirit. It's time to align your heart with God's heart. There is so much beauty and joy in growing closer to God. You hear Him clearer, you appreciate Him more, you have a greater sense of peace, and you are more cognizant of His presence.

What I have found is that God, the great I Am, is whatever you need in that specific moment in your life. He will be your healer, best friend, lover of your soul and provider, just to name a few. He penetrates circumstances and even alters time for you, creating a moment in history. His omnipotence affords Him the ability to be different things to different people at the same time. Since our lives are in cycles or seasons, we learn new things and expand our knowledge about I Am at different times in our lives.

When you surrender to I Am, life becomes more manageable. Surrender is defined as "to yield or to give up completely." The act of surrendering, the breaking of your stubborn will, began when you were born again. However, this act of yielding didn't end at your salvation, it is a continual process.

In your faith walk you will experience God-awakening moments. Awakening means "an act or movement or becoming suddenly aware of something." This is when God steps out of eternity and manifests His presence in our dimension. Have you ever been in your prayer time and sensed the stillness of God? Have you ever been driving in your car and a spirit of worship overcame you? Have you ever just needed a miracle and God surprised you? These are all God-awakening moments.

Let me share a God-awakening moment with you. A couple of years ago, on a cold winter morning, I went downstairs and surprisingly stepped into a puddle of water. This was not the first time we'd had a flood on our first level. After turning the water off in the house and calling the insurance company, I went to the store to buy jugs of water so we could use them later. On my way back, around 6:00 a.m. that morning, I began to cry out of frustration. As I drove home down the long street, I gazed into the dark starry sky and saw an unusual stream of light that was beaming from Heaven to Earth. It was so prominent in the sky; it seemed like a sign from God that He was with me and everything was going to be alright. After parking at the house, I stood outside gazing at this phenomenon, feeling such a spirit of peace. That was a God-awakening moment for me! Have you ever sensed an awareness of God like that? If not, it's time for a refreshing!

Have you ever experienced a wall in your progress? Maybe there are dead or dry areas in your life that refuse to be regenerated. For example, it seems you can never finish a particular project or get back to college after applying year after year, your prayer life doesn't extend beyond grace or maybe you need a spark in your marriage. In Ezekiel 37:1–20, the children of Israel were held in captivity by the Babylonians, seemingly without any hope. Ezekiel, an Old Testament major prophet, received a vision from God about the restoration of Israel. God showed him a valley of dry bones and told him to prophesy to them.

Prophesy means "to utter by divine inspiration, to predict with assurance or to speak as if divinely inspired." When Ezekiel spoke, by faith, to the dry bones, they begin rattling, connecting one to another; then the flesh covered the bones. However, the restored bodies were still lying lifeless. Therefore, Ezekiel had to prophesy again, a second time. This time he commanded the wind, the spirit of life, to breathe into the bones. Suddenly they arose into a great army!

This vision was about restoration and a rebirth of life. Trust that there is nothing in your life that can't be restored or revived. If nothing is impossible with God, there is nothing impossible for you! That means your business idea is possible, the growth of your ministry is possible, your family being reunited is possible, your health being restored is possible, your dream of traveling around the world or buying your first or next home is all possible.

Therefore, I stand with you and declare restoration over your life, including everyone and everything connected to you. Today, you will have to declare or prophesy life over those dead areas as well. And yes, you may have to speak to them more than once! You don't have to walk in the office of a prophet to prophesy. Proverbs 18:21 states that, *"Death and life are in the power of the tongue, and those who love it will eat its fruit."* You have the power to begin restoration and it begins in your confession and declaration. Today, boldly speak forth, by faith, what God has already spoken about you. Then walk in expectation of its manifestation! I will stand in agreement with you.

Keep hoping for it empowers the newness of life. Although new beginnings may seem threatening, you'll soon realize they are the best thing that could happen to you. In this season of expansion, unexpected doors will open for you. You will meet people and go places you have never dreamed of before. There will be an expansion of miracles and fruitful ideas. If you believe it, you will see it! It's time!

"Watch closely. I am preparing something new; it's happening now, even as I speak, and you're about to see it. I am preparing a way through the desert; Waters will flow where there had been none."

(Isaiah 43:19, The Voice)

Chapter 5

Refresh Your Life by Exercising Gratefulness and Grace

One Thanksgiving, I was having a difficult time walking in joy. Many things were transpiring around me that overwhelmed me all at once, causing much discouragement. After reading a devotional, I was inspired to begin a journal of things I was thankful for, from the smallest thing to the largest, from the sun shining to my salvation. I kept up this task for one full year. What an incredible experience and revelation! It helped me see how blessed I was and it opened my eyes to the promises of God that I benefited from on a regular basis. Even if I didn't have everything I thought I "wanted", I had so much to be grateful for. It further conveyed how much I used to complain; it was an old habit that I'm glad came to light.

If you need to feel refreshed again, begin walking in a spirit of thanksgiving. Having a heart of thanksgiving is a daily, conscious and intentional act that keeps your focus on God and reminds you of what truly is important. Being thankful is being appreciative and it is an act of faith, for at times you are thanking God for something that hasn't come to pass yet.

As a result, you must be mindful of what you think about and what you say. Our thoughts and our words affect our demeanor, our spirits, our outlook and even the success of our day. It all begins when you wake up. In the morning, purposely make a decision to thank God and give Him glory for your life.

Through thanksgiving you will find joy and peace in your day, even if you are thanking God through your tears. When you are in a tough place, it can be difficult being grateful. However, this is the most crucial time to take the focus off you. It's helpful if you can connect with someone who will pray with you and encourage you. Isolation steals your ability to be grateful for you are alone with your own thoughts and the enemy has an open door to distract you. When you are being challenged, this is not the time to stop fellowshipping. We all need the unity of the saints in corporate fellowship.

David learned how to encourage himself by stirring his own soul in Psalm 103. He reminded himself of the blessings of God and honored God for His goodness. David commanded his soul to give God praise! We too have to take spiritual authority over our lives and situations. We have to command ourselves to prioritize God in our lives until it becomes an unconscious act. *"Bless the Lord, O my soul; And all that is within me, bless His holy name."* (Psalm 103:1).

Through thanksgiving grace is magnified! Grace is the internal divine strength of God to do something that you can't naturally do on your own; grace is His unmerited favor. It gives us the ability to stand and to believe. Grace does not rely on natural circumstances or natural skills. Through grace you can see from a new perspective and with visions of hope. Grace will empower you to move forward, past the doubt and uncertainty that try to invade your soul. God's grace finds the good in us and helps us see others through the redemptive lens of Christ, through grace eyes.

Grace is the spiritual strength to fulfill your purpose, complete your assignment for the day or to walk through a particular challenge you are facing. We all need the grace of God! Hebrews 4:16 says, *"Let us therefore come boldly to the throne of grace, that we may obtain mercy and find grace to help in time of need."* Sometimes, when you need strength, you don't go to the source of that strength due to shame or unbelief. God's mercy beckons you to Him!

I hope you know by now you can't live successfully in this earth without the grace of God. His favor covers you, empowers you, sustains you and revives your inner being. How refreshing to know that you are not on this journey alone; He is right by your side, equally leading you. God has already equipped you to live this one precious life and not just live this life but live it abundantly (John 10:10).

We all need a refreshing of God's grace, regardless of our financial status, marital status or the position we hold in church. You daily encounter so many things that can be overwhelming to deal with. For we live in turbulent times of organizational restructuring, family crises, plagues, illicit sexual exploits, perverse thinking and unholy political figures. These things should draw you to our Savior. Jesus told us in John 16:33 that, *"These things I have spoken to you, that in Me you may have peace. In the world you will have tribulation; but be of good cheer, I have overcome the world."*

Yes, He has already overcome the world! This victorious fact does not negate us from facing and living in this world, but it does empower or grace us to stand. The grace of God will strengthen you when you feel empty, weak or not good enough. When your cup seems low, God's Word will refill you with His impactful promises:

- *"You will keep him in perfect peace, whose mind is stayed on You, because he trusts in You."* (Isaiah 26:3)
- *"The Lord your God in your midst, The Mighty One, will save; He will rejoice over you with gladness, He will quiet you with His love, He will rejoice over you with singing."* (Zephaniah 3:17)
- *"Now to Him who is able to keep you from stumbling, and to present you faultless before the presence of His glory with*

exceeding joy." (Jude 1:24)

God's Word is infused with power and life. When you meditate on the scriptures, it will bring peace, prosperity and success to your situation.

Humility is needed to walk in God's grace. Humility is defined as the "freedom from pride or arrogance." I will state this; if you haven't experienced it yet, life will humble you. Amen! You will face something in life that will bring you to your knees. Something that will make you feel helpless wondering if God has forgotten you:

- A close loved one dies unexpectedly
- You experience a divorce when you thought this love was forever
- An adult child walks away from God
- You become the product of a rift in your church

These are difficult things to experience; however, the grace of God will give you strength to take one more step forward. You may hear a song that encourages you not to give up, you may read a scripture that solidifies your concerns or someone stands in agreement with you in prayer to believe God again. The joy of God's grace!

In everything, we must live with a state of humility so we realize the profound impact of grace in our lives. For without it we would think, in pridefulness, that we have mastered life in our own strength. I Peter 5:6 says, *"Therefore humble yourselves under the mighty hand of God, that He may exalt you in due time."* This is a personal responsibility we must exercise daily.

Grace and humility align with each other, are dependent upon each other. You can't be too proud to ask God for help or forgiveness, to seek prayer or counseling. We were not designed to live as islands or to survive independently in the earth; we are relational beings like God. Mankind needs one another to survive with balance and wholeness.

Humility is refreshing for it takes the pressure off you to figure it out or to perform in your own strength. It brings peace to your soul. The beauty of grace is a gift that you unwrap every day, filled with the wonders and power of God, reminding you to be grateful for one more chance! Grace reminds you that your life is interwoven with the Creator. And as long as you are connected to Him, you can't fail! As long as you are grateful, God will refresh your spirit and your smile every day!

"But because God was so gracious, so very generous, here I am! And I'm not about to let His grace go to waste."

(1 Corinthians 15:10, *The Message*)

Chapter 6

Refresh Your Life by Experiencing God's Presence

The presence of God! Throughout the Bible, God's presence is manifested in remarkable ways. Moses experienced the presence of God on Mount Horeb (Sinai). And God told him, *"Do not draw near this place. Take your sandals off your feet, for the place where you stand is holy ground"* (Exodus 3:5). When David brought back the Ark of the Covenant (the presence of God) to the City of David, he danced before the Lord with all of his might (II Samuel 6:14). Additionally, in the New Testament, the disciples experienced the presence of God in the flesh through Christ and in the Upper Room through the outpouring of the Holy Spirit (Acts

2:1–4).

How have you experienced the presence of God? You will know His presence without a shadow of doubt, for His presence is tangible. It can manifest sweetly or strong as a rushing wind! How precious are those times when you are able to bask in His love and His undeniable peace. During moments like these, you may find tears flowing from your eyes or a smile appear on your face for no reason at all.

But have you ever felt a disconnect from His presence? If so, don't fear; He has not left your side. God is an ever-present and on-time help in our lives. He is Emmanuel; God with us! You see Him in creation; you hear Him in a song; you feel Him in your heart and in a hug and you sense Him in your loved one's voice saying, "I love you." God's presence is always available to the humble heart, to the one who is enthralled with His loyal love!

Psalm 121:1 & 2 reminds us of the mighty power and presence of God. *"I will lift up my eyes to the hills from whence cometh my help? My help comes from the Lord, who made heaven and earth."* I've always admired God's creation. Seeing and hearing the ocean, driving under large trees with the warm-colored leaves cascading over the car or admiring the varied shapes of clouds in the vast blue sky. Creation effortlessly magnifies God's awesomeness, His majestic presence and creativity. Creation proclaims His name loudly and without apology!

When I lived in Southern California, our family lived in the San Bernardino Valley with mountains right behind our home.

What a heavenly sight to see every day. When I looked upon the mountains, it reminded me to keep my head lifted up, past the distractions and even when things didn't make any sense. On rare occasions, I would go up to the mountains to view the city below. The air was clean and brisk up there. The clouds seemed only a touch away. In this atmosphere, you just felt closer to God!

We tend to get so busy and forget to stop and appreciate the beauty of God's creation and His magnificent splendor. Who is like the Lord? Who compares with Him? No one, so take time to enjoy His beauty that surrounds you. With each breath, appreciate life in His presence.

God's presence exudes His unconditional love. What is refreshing about God's love?

- Knowing that you are redeemed and have an Advocate who constantly prays for you.
- Knowing that He loved you before you accepted Him. He desired you even when you felt unwanted or unloved. He chose you in the Beloved!
- Knowing that He forgives you of your sins, past, present and future, and still has a plan for your life.

Experiencing God's presence must be a priority in your life. There is a song by Larnell Harris (Album: *From a Servant's Heart*, 1987) entitled "I Miss My Time with You." The chorus lyrics are:

"I miss my time with you, those moments together. I need to be with

you each day, and it hurts me when you say you're too busy, busy trying to serve me, but how can you serve me when your spirit's empty? There's a longing in my heart, wanting more than just a part of you. It's true; I miss my time with you."

The words of that song really make you ponder and think about if you are spending quality time with Abba Father. It's amazing that the omnipotent God, the Alpha and Omega, who designed every flower, who breathed life into our mortal bodies and knitted you in your mother's womb desires to commune with you—to be in relationship with you, to fellowship or have Koinonia with you. Koinonia is Greek for "communion or joint participation." Truly we are connected to God. Luke said it so eloquently in Acts 17:28: *"For in Him we live and move and have our being, as some of your own poets have said, 'For we are also His offspring.'"* We even take Communion on a regular basis because of our covenant with God and to commemorate the death and life of His Son, Jesus Christ, solidifying we are one with God.

Psalm 91:1 speaks of a secret place in the Most High. This is a place where we are safe in His presence. This secret place is a vulnerable place; nothing is hidden from God. Even your inner thoughts He knows. The areas of your life where you have been hiding brokenness or hurt are now open. Even the things we are not proud of that we performed in our past that nobody knows about are open to Him. This can be an uncomfortable place. But it's also a place of liberation! The secret place beckons you to come, rest and lay your head upon your Abba Father's lap. It's a place of hope, cleansing, joy and remarkable peace.

In the secret place, we must cast upon Him our past hurts from life so we can receive healing from:

- The time one of your parents left and never came back—it's time to release it!
- When the engagement went south and you had to call off the wedding—it's time to release it!
- When your dreams were shattered because of a sports accident and now you have to reframe your future—it's time to release it!

It's time to let it go! You've been holding yourself back long enough. Let's break the chain of disappointment and create positive memories. Dream new dreams, open your heart to love one more time, or revive another skill. God's power within you will allow you to begin again.

The presence of God must be sought after. Yes, seeking God is a spiritual discipline! That connection comes through prayer, which is a two-way line of communication with God. In prayer we have the ability to:

- Glorify God and thank Him for His goodness.
- Activate the promises of God in the earth.
- Intercede for others. As my pastors say, "There's no distance in the spirit."
- Receive direction from God. Find peace with decisions you

have to make.

Our desire for God dwelt in our hearts before we were saved. It was that still small voice that drew us, igniting our hearts when we received Jesus Christ as our personal Savior! In every person there is a longing, a hunger for God, even if we don't know it. That emptiness pulls at you and nags at you desiring to be filled even by the wrong things. When we feel this emptiness, we must seek Him and bypass all of the distractions this world offers. The world will tell you that you aren't successful in your arena if you are not working 60 hours a week or climbing the corporate ladder. Society emphasizes that you need more and bigger things. However, nothing can substitute for knowing and abiding with God.

After you've experienced His presence, the sense of awe, the incredible peace that fills the room or His tangible love, you desire Him more and more and you know you unequivocally can't live without Him. His presence transforms you, making you more like Him. Nothing on this earth can substitute for God's presence. *"Where can I go from Your Spirit? Or where can I flee from Your presence?"* (Psalm 139:7).

The Bible displays the presence of God the Father, Jesus and the Holy Spirit in every book of the Bible. I won't share every book; however, I want to give you a glimpse of the power of His presence that exudes through God's love letters (courtesy of Philip Nation from Bible Study Tools):

- Genesis – Creator and promised Redeemer
- Joshua – Commander of the army of the Lord

- Ruth – Our Kinsman, Redeemer
- 1 Chronicles – Son of David who is coming to rule
- Esther – Protector of the people
- Proverbs – Our wisdom
- Daniel – The stranger in the fire with us
- Matthew- The Messiah who is King
- Acts – The Spirit who dwells in His people
- Ephesians – The unity of the church
- 2 Thessalonians – Our returning King
- Hebrews – Our High Priest
- Revelation – The King of Kings and Lord of Lords

God is omnipresent, from eternity past to eternity future. In all His vastness, He promised that He would be with you in eternity present, any time you need Him. You can count on His Word! We serve a mighty God! He is the one who will move Heaven and earth for you. What a revelation that He loves to be with you, yes YOU! As Psalm 100 declares, we are to come into His presence with singing and enter His courts with thanksgiving. It's a privilege to have access to the Holy One, to the King of Glory. You can't take this honor lightly, son and daughter of the King. You're invited to be refreshed in His presence today!

"You will show me the path of life; In Your presence is Fullness of joy; At Your right hand are pleasures forevermore."

(Psalm 16:11)

REFRESHING

Chapter 7

Refresh Your Life by Declaring God's Strength

The world tells us we do not need anyone's help or guidance; that we can do this life without anyone's intervention. We are intelligent beings and can forge our own paths, right? We can climb the corporate ladder, take care of families and fulfill every goal all in our own strength. However, that is not a realistic perception, is it? We were not created to manage life alone or sustain our living in isolation. God knew that we would need spiritual assistance. When Jesus ascended into Heaven after His resurrection, He sent the Holy Spirit to indwell believers, then and now. The Holy Spirit in the Greek means "paraklete", translated as "helper". He is our comforter, teacher and reminder of God's Word and through the Holy Spirit we are able to operate in the supernatural! The Holy

Spirit's help and strength may go unnoticed in our lives because He is intricately involved in every aspect of our day.

Nevertheless, there may have been times in your life when you felt helpless or felt lost without any power. We all have experienced those unforgettable moments. Life will bring those difficult times when we least expect it; these moments get etched in our memory. I recall when my father unexpectedly passed in February 1997, my heart was broken and I could literally feel the emptiness encompassing me. So I wouldn't lose my mind, I had to quickly resolve in my heart that the only way to get through this time was for God to be my source of strength and to daily fill the void that was too painful to experience.

In those life-altering moments, when we can't see how to move forward, we must understand that God is omnipotent! He has ALL power in His hands. He reigns over all the heavens and the earth. He is Sovereign, He is our Rock, He is our Healer and He is our Deliverer. Psalm 24:8 declares, *"Who is this King of glory? The Lord strong and mighty, The Lord mighty in battle."* God alone is the only one we can completely lean on. He is the only one who can bear the weight of our burdens. Do you know that popular song by Bill Withers (1972) "Lean on Me"? He wasn't talking about the Lord, but he sure got the lyrics right: *Lean on me, when you're not strong, and I'll be your friend, I'll help you carry on.* Jesus is that friend. He is our true companion (John 15:14 & 15). How many things has God carried you through?

Some days we all need strength (capacity to endure) just

to get out of bed, to go to work, and to get through a long day. Life can zap energy right out of you! Have you ever been tired physically, emotionally or even mentally? And all at the same time! Good news! God's strength is not beyond your grasp. Nehemiah 8 shares that the joy of the Lord is your strength. God is never without joy for He embodies joy. We can receive constant gladness from Him.

Isaiah 40:31 proclaims that God will renew you with eagle's strength. The eagle's strength is an "above the storm" strength, a new lease of life strength, and a new altitude strength. God will provide this renewed strength to walk through and overcome obstacles as you wait on Him. Waiting is a verb, an action word. How are you waiting on the Lord? Impatiently, complaining or with a heart of service? I've discovered that waiting is not idleness but active service. This is a time to enhance the Kingdom of God while you wait for your manifestation.

To obtain a renewed strength is to admit your current human strength is frail and not enough. What a humbling revelation! But it's a necessary discovery to walk in the power, grace and strength of God. This refreshing moment comes when you finally surrender to casting all your cares upon the Lord and releasing yourself from bearing it all. This is a continual task that you must exercise to obtain peace and balance.

Carrying the load of your family or your own problems is just too much for anyone to bear. God did not create you to carry the cares of the world on your shoulders. With this burden comes:

- Stress – "A state of mental or emotional strain or tension resulting from adverse or demanding circumstances." Stress comes in different forms and can debilitate you with physical ailments and emotional outbursts.
- Impatience – This is when you are quick to anger and insensitive towards others. The Word explains that anger does not produce the righteousness of God.
- Weariness – This is when you are physically, mentally and emotionally tired. This position puts a strain on your relationships and your work. Weariness makes it difficult to keep balance and peace within you and home. The "superman" or "superwoman" syndrome also brings weariness; you lose focus on your reliance on God. Your time and energy are allocated to surviving and not trusting Him.
- Worry – A sense of fear and foreboding thoughts that overwhelm you and bring anxiousness to the level of not being able to concentrate, eat or sleep. Worrying is not God's will for your life.

As caregivers and heads of households, you want the best for you family, you want all of their needs met, and you want your children to accomplish more than you did in your life. Be cautious not to think that you are their sole provider, the center of their universe. No one can take the place of Jehovah Jireh, our provider, the All-Sufficient One. Rest in this truth!

In Joshua chapter 1, God shared with Joshua about his new leadership role with the Israelites. In verse nine, God commanded Joshua to be strong and courageous and not to fear. In fact, God told him this three times. You will find in life that there are times when you just have to be strong, even when you don't want to stand and even if you feel like you don't have the ability to stand. Stand:

- When your loved one dies and you are arranging all of the funeral plans, not even taking time to grieve.
- When your child is spiritually lost and you have to stand in the gap for him/her again.
- When your company decides it's time to relocate your role or eliminate your position, leaving you unemployed.

Yes, it takes strength to stand and it takes strength to press forward! But as you meditate on God's Word and rely on Him, He strengthens you day by day. With time you will become like a tree planted by the rivers of water (Psalm 1:3)—strong and healthy, able to weather any storm. The tree's roots obtain nourishment and strength from the water, similar to the believer obtaining strength from the Holy Spirit.

As you can see, you must be connected to God to obtain His strength. He waits for you to come to Him, to delight in Him and to confide in Him. It is His strength that restores your heart so you can fulfill your responsibilities and purpose. Accept that you don't have all the answers, you can't fix everything on your own and that you need someone greater than yourself. This is where God wants you; completely reliant upon Him, completely surrendered, receiving His strength. Now you are in a place of refreshing strength!

> *"Always follow the Eternal,*
> *His strength and His face."*
>
> **(1 Chronicles 16:11, The Voice)**

Chapter 8

Refresh Your Life by Recovering Your Peace

When I was growing up, I learned a song entitled "Let There Be Peace on Earth." But how can one obtain peace in these strenuous times? The world is filled with hostility, confusion, pain and competing ideas. The news on television shares more bad information than good information. It can be difficult finding peace when your life is bombarded with images of killing, sickness, hatred, corruption and social unrest. Sometimes you have to just turn off the television and social media.

What is peace? It is defined as "freedom from disturbance or tranquility." Only limited peace can be obtained by earthly measures. Oh, we try to find solutions to having peace, even for a short while, but we know those attempts are all futile. Jesus made it very plain: *"I am leaving you with a gift—peace of mind and heart. And the peace I give is a gift the world cannot give. So, don't be troubled or afraid"* (NLT). True peace can only be found in God! Isaiah 26:3 shares, *You will keep him in perfect peace, whose mind is stayed on You, because he trusts in You.* We have a responsibility to look to God for peace for only He embodies and reflects it in completion.

Peace is so refreshing! It's such a rare commodity but one that can be achieved. Life is constantly demanding something from you with its competing priorities. Therefore, you have to learn to capture peace; more importantly, dwell in it every day. In time you'll learn that peace is not the absence of problems but the grace to release those problems to God without worry, frustration or fear. You have to learn how to turn off your mind and stop trying to figure it all out so you can embrace your peace. Ouch! That stepped on my own toes. God only operates in faith. Your role is to find scriptures that minister to your need and meditate on them; proclaim them until peace rests upon you.

Sometimes solitude brings peace. Yes, solitude can be refreshing! Don't be afraid to take some time alone and hear yourself breathe or think. Psalm 46:10 states, *"Be still, and know that I am God."* To reemphasize this verse, let's look at this verse in the New American Standard Bible. It plainly states, *Cease striving and know that I am God.* That means STOP what you're doing! Stop worrying, stop complaining, and stop overextending yourself. Learn to rest! Enjoy some time of self-care.

Peace gives you uninterrupted time to reflect, be restored

and even dream. This may be a hard task to accomplish, but hopefully you can carve time out for yourself. In doing so you can reconnect with God as you pour your heart out to Him and abide in His peace. It's okay to let your tears flow. It releases the pressure of always being on. *"You have taken account of my wanderings; Put my tears in Your bottle. Are they not recorded in Your book?" (*Psalm 56:9, AMP). Abba Father is always available to you!

And if you can't accomplish a "me-retreat" get up 30 minutes earlier than your family. While the house is quiet, bask in God's peace. And in these moments of stillness, I love to talk to God, but more importantly I love to be quiet and listen. God shares scriptures and songs with me and encompasses me with His presence.

What brings you peace? There's nothing like a peaceful afternoon when it's raining outside or riding quietly in the car admiring God's handiwork all around you. Peace comes in different forms and is obtained in unique ways:

- You may enjoy working on a project in the garage.
- Listening to soft instrumental music.
- Meditating and praying.
- Cooking a feast for your family.
- Sitting with a friend having an in-depth conversation.

I encourage you to take advantage of these refreshing, peaceful moments or what best ministers to your heart. Here is a sample affirmation for you to declare (there are more affirmations in the *Time of Application* section in the back).

Affirmation of Peace: My mind will only dwell on things that affect eternity, things above the earth not on the earth. What could that include?

- Things that give God the glory.
- Prayers of intercession.
- Words of encouragement.
- Declarative faith statements.

The power of peace is the power to surrender! A time to say, "God, I can't do this by myself." Life can be overwhelming! However, God encourages you to come to Him boldly and cast all of your care upon Him. He will perfect (make right) all those things that concern you. Yes, He cares about everything in your life, even the little things. *How am I going to pay this bill? When will I meet my soul mate? Where did I put those keys?* (Smile). He appreciates you coming to Him with everything.

It takes discipline to keep your mind off your troubles, your family's troubles and the cares of the day. Philippians 4:6 shares, *"Be anxious (uneasy or worried) for nothing, but in everything by prayer and supplication, with thanksgiving, let your requests be made known to God."* Therefore, you have to trust Him and walk by faith and not by your natural elements.

As you trust Him, the anxiety of life decreases so peace can abound. As you trust Him, fear subsides so you can function effectively. As you trust Him, life's worries dissipate; a spirit of calmness soothes you. Cherish your moments of peace; it is necessary to remaining sane. That's right! Our enemy will have you think that you are going crazy. You are not, my friend! Just refresh your mind with God's promises and command a sweet rest tonight!

"We ask You, Eternal One, to give strength to your people; Eternal One, bless them with the gift of peace."

(Psalm 29:11, The Voice)

REFRESHING

Chapter 9

Refresh Your Life by Walking Out Your Faith

Faith! The ability to believe something that you cannot see with expectation of its fruition. Here's how Hebrews 11:1 describes faith: *"Faith shows the reality of what we hope for; it is the evidence of things we cannot see."* (NLT). This may seem strange considering we live in this natural world, a world that we experience with our physical senses every day. But as a believer, faith is the realm in which we dwell and thrive. Why do we need faith? Because we believe in God who we can't see or even understand His very existence. Our salvation is based on faith; without it, our relationship with Christ is in vain. We need faith to operate in the spirit world where we have been given authority to dwell in heavenly places.

Nevertheless, we live on this side of Heaven and our faith

can waver at times; health issues challenge us, worry can weigh us down, and family problems can seem endless. Life can be distorted when you operate out of emotions or your eyesight is too low. You have to constantly and purposely, *"Set your mind on things above, not on things on the earth"* (Colossians 3:2). If you are led by your senses you will not operate in faith and will lose focus on God's best for you.

Faith bypasses emotions and relies on the foundation of the Word of God. Faith sees forward to what will be, for what will be will manifest in the present when you believe! Our faith is that powerful! Yet emotions will distract you from your destiny for they operate through feelings that are temporary and short-sighted. These senses are not reliable, leaving you with false truths and insecurities.

- Do I have what it takes?
- Who will accept my ministry?
- Is this really God's will for my life?
- I'm afraid to try something new.

Do not allow the voices to distract you and sway your faith. Be encouraged; God can restore or strengthen your faith! This will require you to let go of your past and what you can comprehend and trust God's heart and His character. God's heart says, "You are my daughter and son and I will never give up on you. You can believe me to take you to the next level." God's character says, "I love you and nothing can separate you from my plan for you." His love will fill you with His confidence.

So, know that you are not wandering around aimlessly; you are not lost or confused. God has called you! Amen! God has already gone before you and prepared the way. You can be confident that your steps are ordered by Him. Philippians 1:6 states, *"Being confident of this very thing, that He who has begun a good work in you will complete it until the day of Jesus Christ."* God is at work in you; now faith forward!

Today, I challenge you with this question: do you have a faith project you're working on? I encourage you to have at least one faith project you're working on to keep you invigorated. It will stretch your faith, fulfill you, help others and ultimately give God the glory. Faith projects are an opportunity for growth and if it doesn't challenge you, it's not big enough. Tell me, how will you know the greater things God has for you if you don't stretch yourself? If you stay in your comfort zone, you will never see the manifested power of God. His power that works in you is immeasurable (indefinitely extensive).

Faith projects are projects that you can't figure out. You may have only a glimpse of the project's totality and that's it. Faith projects will grip you, calling your name; beckoning you into the deep.

It is time for you to take a leap of faith or, as I call it, Casting the Net! Let me explain; after Christ's resurrection, the disciples went back to their vocations. One night, the experienced fishermen fished all night long and were unsuccessful. Christ saw them from the beach and told them to cast their net to the right side or to the other side of the boat. They conceded to His command and caught more fish than they could carry. The fish represented souls they would catch through their ministry.

What else does this passage tell us? Sometimes you just have to try again; there is greater beyond your reach. You can't give up too quickly on the dreams or goals you've set. Sometimes you get so stuck in your ways you can't see beyond the obvious. You get comfortable with your fears to such a degree that you don't take the leap of faith into the deep. I agree that there can be a fear of the unknown and a fear of failure. If you can't control something, you are intimated by it. However, this is not God's will for you. You need the favor of God, the grace of His Son and the power of the Holy Spirit to conquer your fear.

Today, you have to solidify in your heart and mind that you either will believe God or you will not. Yes, it's that simple! Because without faith it's impossible to please God. This can be challenging, don't get me wrong. When confusion is all around and things don't add up, it's easy to forget that even though we live in the flesh, we operate in the spirit. And it's in the spirit where we are victorious! *"For the weapons of our warfare are* not carnal but mighty in God for pulling down strongholds" (2 Corinthians 10:4).

The key to faith is that it requires action. You've heard the scripture from James 2:17 that states, *"The same is true with faith. Without actions, faith is useless. By itself,* it's *as good as* dead" (The Voice). So it's not enough to believe that your dreams or goals will come to pass. You have to partner with God and partake in the fulfillment of them as well. As you read and ponder on the Word of God, your faith will expand giving you the ability to stretch. *"So then faith comes by hearing, and hearing by the word of God"* (Romans 10:17). This is a continual task! Now you have to take action then call your promise or dream into the earth realm.

The Bible states that your latter days will be greater than your past. I believe this is true because as you grow in your relationship with God you mature, you learn more about His nature and what He desires for you. With time you gain greater insight when you apply His promises to your life. This activates your faith, leading to greater manifestations. Moreover, you learn not to allow fear and uncertainty to control your future, which opens the door to greater possibilities. You can be confident in your future because God is already there, leading you to it. Our God is a progressive God, a moving forward God. He desires that you continually grow in your spiritual journey.

Philippians 2:13 shares that God will give you the will and ability to do His good pleasure. There is purpose for each of your days! Your responsibility is to allow faith to do its work in you. God has given you the ability to call things from Heaven to Earth. Now walk with an expectation that every day you will see God's hand move on your behalf. What a refreshing and transforming perspective to live by!

"Watch, stand fast in the faith, be brave, be strong!"
(1 Corinthians 16:13)

REFRESHING

Chapter 10

Refresh Your Life by Understanding the Vision

Vision: the act or power of seeing. Read how the Word of God encourages us: *"Then the Lord answered me and said: Write the vision and make it plain on tablets, that he may run who reads it. For the vision is yet for an appointed time; but at the end it will speak, and it will not lie. Though it tarries, wait for it; because it will surely come, it will not tarry."* (Habakkuk 2:2 & 3). The only way to write the vision is to know the vision. Do you know what God has desired for you in this season? What beckons you? I mean this dream won't go away. You think about it every day with excitement. When you operate in it, you are passionate and energetic and you know you are operating out of purpose. You know that God is pleased! Joy fills your heart knowing you are doing the will of Father God and giving Him glory in your life. Even when you're challenged by the vision, you keep pursuing it. That is your vision!

However, what do you do when you know your vision but are not seeing it come to pass? Fulfilling your vision can be like a plane that is operating in a strategic holding pattern. What is a strategic holding pattern? First let's define these two words:

- Strategic: a long-term or overall interest to achieve, a carefully, thoughtfully designed plan.

- Holding pattern: a flight path or route maintained by an aircraft awaiting permission or clearance to land or it is a state of waiting.

A strategic holding pattern is a waiting place, a place of transition, before the plan is manifested, which means you are in an "in between" state. The formal definition of transition is the process or a period of changing from one state to another. Is anyone in transition today? Are you between unemployment and employment? Singleness and marriage? Brokenness and healing?

Companies, large and small, keep their employees motivated and empowered with a vision statement. The C-suite executives make strategic plans, usually three to five years out. In the plans they lay out company goals that align with the company's vision and mission and how they will accomplish them. The strategic plan is used as a focal point for employees to keep them informed and moving forward. Likewise, each of us has a strategic plan, from God, for our lives. We need to write the plan out or write the dream down so we have a visual focal point, motivating us to keep pressing forward.

How do you manage between your dream and its manifestation? What do you do when you begin to get tired, even doubting that the dream was for you? While you're waiting, your role is to believe the dream, seek God, prepare and expect!

Believing is paramount; without a vision you will perish in unbelief! Without your faith, you will not receive the dream, you will not fulfill your purpose. Hebrews 11:6 states, *"But without faith it is impossible to please Him, for he who comes to God must believe that He is, and that He is a rewarder of those who diligently seek Him."* That sounds like your faith is a mandatory ingredient in vision manifestation!

Furthermore, as you seek God, He will reveal His plans for you. He will reveal your next steps and connect you to the right people. He will also give you grace and strength to wait (Psalm 37:7). Next you need to prepare for the right opportunity; do what is necessary to be ready. Take the classes, get the passport, write the business plan and meet professionals in your arena. Get ready to implement!

We serve a strategic God! Strategy is defined as "a careful plan or method." God strategically worked in the life of Esther; in the end, she was in the proper position of power and influence to save her people. God strategically worked in Joseph's trials, leading him to become second in command in Egypt, and he was able to save his entire family. God strategically worked in Saul's transformation to Paul. He wrote the majority of the New Testament and served in the expansion of the gospel to the Gentiles. God is also strategically working in your life. He is masterfully coordinating your past, your mistakes, and your connections and bringing them to fruition for your good and at the right time.

God is the master planner; leaving nothing incomplete or to chance including your dreams! Because He is omniscient, he knows your end from the beginning (Isaiah 46:10 & 11). God is so confident in His plan for you that He tells you that, although it tarries, wait for it! Why would He tell you to wait for something that is not coming? God is not a man that He should lie.

You also need to walk with a spirit of expectation. Romans 4:17 tells us we have the power: *"In the presence of Him whom he believed – God, who gives life to the dead and calls those things which do not exist as though they did."* We must profess the end today; we must profess the dream! Truly your manifestation will require your participation!

"Staying in your lane" is a popular quote today and what it means is not getting distracted by what other people are doing, not looking to the left or right (Proverbs 4:25–27). I must tell you that the plan or dream is not always revealed at once, but it is manifested in stages. If you are in a "holding pattern" right now, know that God is guiding you through it. Your life is not stifled. On the contrary, you are actively waiting, progressing forward. It's known that if a runner turns around while running it will slow them down and may even cause them to fall. Don't dwell on the past. You will lose precious time.

We may not always understand the timing of God, but we can trust the character of God, His love, faithfulness, wisdom and grace. Although you may be in a place of transition, He is faithful to perform what He started. God is with you! You are being strategically positioned by God who is not confined by time. Instead, He can alter time for your dream to manifest. That's why you can be assured that the holding pattern comes to an end! The plane completes its strategic pattern and lands at its planned destination. In other words, it reaches the goal of the flight! And so will you! The manifestation of your dreams brings God glory and draws souls to Him. Our dreams give us permission to impart eternity into others' lives.

There's a popular song by gospel artist Anita Wilson entitled "It's Done" (Album – *Worship Soul*, 2012). I love this song for it reminds us that we are already complete and that the goals we are destined to accomplish are already done; you just have to walk them out. Remember we serve the God who is the Alpha and Omega. He is the beginning and ending of our faith, our dreams and our lives.

When you know and fulfill your vision, you are walking in success but not mankind's definition of success. Success is knowing God. Success is doing the will of God. Success is fulfilling your purpose. Success is going beyond the word "no". Success is saying yes when the odds are against you; saying yes to life after a divorce, yes to a new job after being unemployed for a lengthy time, and saying yes to life after a period of depression. I declare today that you are a success!

Your vision is still alive! Muster the strength and courage to write it down then project it vocally. Your vision will revive a spark in you. It will give you renewed purpose! It will guide your plans and your actions. Identify what you can begin today and what you can do tomorrow and it will come to fruition. And it's okay if you have to revise your vision from time to time. Like you, it's a work in progress!

"But if we hope for what we do not see, we eagerly wait for it with perseverance."

(Romans 8:25)

Chapter 11

Refresh Your Life by Creating an Atmosphere of Worship

God created us to know Him and to worship Him! Inside every human being's heart is a void that only can be filled by our living Creator. We all used to drift through life looking for things to fill us and complete us. We lived beneath our potential and settled for relationships and situations that were not healthy for us. Then, one day, our souls said, "Yes," and we responded to the call that had beckoned us all our lives. With this enlightenment our desires turned to honoring and knowing God. What came from this heavenly encounter was worship.

Worship! It is defined as "ascribing worth to someone or

something" or "the feeling or expression of reverence and adoration for a deity." God is worthy of our worship! The Book of Psalms is also known as the *Book of Praises* and the leading author was King David, with 73 chapters penned by him. On the rolling green hills, David the shepherd would worship God through song and poetry. As you read through the chapters he wrote in Psalms, you can feel his heart, his passion and his pain from his life journey. His poetic words connect with anyone's heart through chapters like: 23, 34, 51, 103 or 139.

Yet worship began before the foundations of the earth. Before eternity past, the angels worshipped God and to this day they continue to give Him the highest praise. Hallelujah is the highest form of praise and is a word "used to express praise, joy or thanks." Biblically the definition of hallelujah means "Praise the Lord!" Declare hallelujah in the morning! Declare hallelujah in the afternoon! Declare hallelujah in the evening. Hallelujah!

Our worship to God is so powerful, rejuvenating and absolutely necessary for mankind's existence. It's powerful because it aligns our hearts and situations to God's Word and declares all things are under our feet and the name of Jesus. It's rejuvenating because when we magnify God, we make Him bigger than ourselves. Your focus on Him alleviates all of your worries leaving you with a spirit of joy. Our worship is necessary because of who He is. God is:

- Adonai – Hebrew name for God is my Lord
- El Shaddai – Lord God Almighty

- Yahweh – Hebrew name for God
- Jehovah Rapha – The Lord that heals
- Jehovah Shalom – The Lord is peace

God is everything! He deserves our glory and reverence.

You want to feel refreshed—sing a song, listen to some instrumental worship or sing around the house. You see your worship allows you to have a place in God that the enemy used to occupy. It will give you a position of authority in the spirit. So, you must keep your focus, maintain your posture, continue to lift up your voice, and see the hand of the Lord work on your behalf!

How do you create an atmosphere of worship? First of all, people worship in many fashions, through:

- Singing
- Praying and meditating
- Dancing
- Reading God's Word
- Lifting of hands

Although our forms of worship vary, as long as it's done with a pure heart, God will be honored. Nevertheless, worship is not just singing or praising God. Worship is a lifestyle. Your day-to-day activities should honor God. Have you ever found yourself praying as you're washing the dishes or driving somewhere? Worship tunes you to God's frequency, aligning your will with His will. When you worship God, you put Him above all concerns. When you decrease, you focus on God's traits and His character, which in return elevates your own thoughts. We operate our worship in faith, activating God's Word in the supernatural and calling it forth to the natural.

Your worship brings forth breakthrough and deliverance in your life and in the lives of others! The angels perform God's Word when they hear it (Psalm 103:21), but you must have the faith to put forth God's Word in the atmosphere. For if you do, that's when things change; restoration and miracles come forth and favor is manifested! This is the power of worship!

Our worship will bring forth joy in our lives, refreshment in our souls, strength in our bodies and peace in our minds. Worship manifests the power of God! Worship keeps you grounded, balanced and is a calming of your soul. Worship transcends your thoughts and emotions and bestows upon you a heavenly peace.

In addition, worship is a weapon of power that will fight for you. In the Old Testament, when the armies came against Israel and King Jehoshaphat, God ministered through Jahaziel, a Levite. He encouraged them with these words: "the battle is not yours but the Lord's." Even though the battle was fixed they still had to position themselves and worship God to see the salvation of the Lord manifested. When the praises of Judah and Jerusalem went forth, their worship was an act of faith, causing their enemies to fight each other; defeating one another (2 Chronicles 20:17–22). Their worship to God gave them the victory! That is powerful!

Furthermore, worship is a weapon of prayer that avails in

the spirit! Avail means "to produce or result as a benefit." Therefore, your worship produces results that will benefit you and all that are connected to you. Worship stirs your soul and activates faith in you. Worship declares to the enemy that no matter what it looks like, you have the victory!

Lastly, we are commanded to worship God. Psalm 150:6 states, *"Let everything that has breath praise the Lord. Praise the Lord!"* Even when you don't feel like worshiping, you have to muster the strength to honor God, even through your tears. It's called a sacrifice of praise. This press ultimately strengthens and refreshes you.

Since the Spirit of God lives in you, you have the power to create an atmosphere of worship wherever you go—in your home, your car and even at work. When you worship God, you invite Him into your situation and into your life right then and there. His presence is greater than any negative feeling, discouragement or negative report. So, don't let your feelings hinder your victory! Worship God in sincerity, in spirit and in truth. It's your rightful and inherited position.

"Give to the Lord the glory due His name; Bring an offering, and come Before Him. Oh, worship the Lord in the beauty of holiness!"

(1 Chronicles 16:29)

REFRESHING

Chapter 12

Refresh Your Life by Remembering Who You Are

"*But you are a chosen generation, a royal priesthood, a holy nation, His own special people, that you may proclaim praises of Him who called you out of darkness into His marvelous light.*" (I Peter 2:9). Yes, you are a peculiar person, set aside for the purpose and glory of God! This means you are not going to fit in everywhere you go and that's okay. Let's break down this scripture:

- Peculiar means – "odd, unusual or special"
- Holy means – "set apart for a divine purpose"

How refreshing learning to be your own unique self, not

competing or comparing yourself to anyone. How empowering to know that God chose you and ordained your days before there were any. Be grateful for your path or journey of life, it is not by happenstance. It is purposeful! So, stop the comparisons right now! There is no one else like you. Your specific gifts are needed in the earth, in your community and in your family.

Nor has God forgotten about you! He has a special plan for you and it will not align with what your neighbor or co-worker is doing. Remember God's thoughts are not your thoughts and His ways are not your ways (Isaiah 55:8 & 9). You think you are being left out but you're not. Your path is orchestrated for a higher calling. In fact, your journey doesn't even make sense to you sometimes, but it does to God. And although you may not fully understand His plan, it does not negate that there is a plan. A divine master plan is in order and your future is waiting for you.

The devil is subtle with his lies and messages to you. You cannot allow him to make you feel condemned or less than anyone else. That mindset limits you and distracts you from your true purpose. It hinders your progress and mobility. You're mandated to speak God's Word over you and your family and it will silence the lies and negative messaging. Speak life, intercessor! Speak peace! Speak hope!

Have you ever wondered why you were put in your particular family? It was for a strategic purpose. First, your life is a light to your family, your life is an encouragement to them and your life is an example of Christ before them. Yes, you are meant to go against the grain and the family traditions. You're meant to stand out and to be the odd one! I mean you've already learned how to march to a different drum.

As you fulfill your dreams of entrepreneurship, world traveling, as an inventor and even a millionaire, your family will not be surprised. Adventures are not new to you and they're defined as "an unusual and exciting experience." You've actually have had many escapades already:

- You started a new career when your old job seemed sufficient.
- You moved out of state when people thought it didn't make sense.
- You stepped out into ministry and accepted the calling on your life when it seemed safer to stay in the background.
- You launched your own business when the economy said, "Not now."

Adventures are faith experiences that you walk out. Therefore, you can't stop now! Even though you are in a different place in life, with greater responsibilities, there is still adventure in you. It's time to rebirth your adventurous spirit. What's hindering you?

You, my friend, are complete in Christ! You are healed physically, emotionally and within your mind. You are no longer held by your past. Your present is a product of your faith and your future is filled with greatness! You are a prayer warrior and understand the power of prayer. James 5:16 states, *"The effective, fervent prayer of a righteous avails much."* Continue to pray and intercede; it does make a difference.

Remember you are built for the challenge and have the ability to complete the task. God has begun a good work in you; He has equipped you for every adventure of faith before you. Are you tackling school as an adult learner? Have you set up the appointment at the Small Business Administration Office? Is it time to start your ministry? Are you signing the papers on your rental home? That's awesome! Don't allow fear to deter you. Your confidence is not in yourself, it is in the power of the Holy Spirit that dwells in you. God has given you courage and the strength to accomplish all of your goals.

Proverbs 23:7 states, *"For as he thinks in his heart, so is he."* You are a mighty man and woman of valor! You sit in heavenly places! You are anointed! Don't devalue or disqualify the anointing in your life and the indwelling of the Holy Spirit. How precious it is! You are valuable because you were made in the image of God and you were especially formed, in totality, by His hands. God has crowned you His with glory and honor. You are blessed!

As humans we have the tendency to look for affirmations from others, whether that is from our parents, spouse, children, or manager. It's natural that we desire to belong, to receive attention and to be loved. Ephesians 1:6 reminds us that we are accepted in the Beloved. You already belong to a divine and eternal family.

Psalm 92:4–5 emphasizes the greatness of God's work. I believe this is not just speaking about creation, but God is addressing the greatness in you! With all that said, if no one has told you lately, "You are doing an awesome job! Thank you for taking care of your family! Thank you for not giving up!"

In addition, you must take time to celebrate yourself! Thank God for the intermediate steps and do not neglect the day of small beginnings (Zechariah 4:10). Dynamic work always begins with a seed. Right now, enjoy the journey as your ministry or business grows.

Here are a few suggestions to assist you in celebrating yourself:

- Give God praise for using you in this season.
- Invite friends who support your vision to dinner.
- Celebrate the small milestones within the greater goal. On your project board, move your accomplished tasks to the "Completed" column so you can visibly see your successes.
- Declare the blessing of God over you!
- Appreciate and value who God created you to be! Identify your strengths and areas you want to improve in.

Knowing your strengths is a sign of leadership. Leadership: "the act of motivating a group of people to achieve a common goal." You don't have to be in management to be a leader. By being a believer, you are a natural leader! We all know that leadership is not for the faint of heart; having the ability to influence others is a serious responsibility.

Leadership of others is an honor that may be bestowed upon you in various seasons of your life. To be able to empower others to be their very best or lead them to success is not a small or menial feat. With leadership come qualities like responsibility, humbleness and eyes of grace. However, on the other side of the coin comes the pressure of others' lives being influenced by you. This must be managed effectively or it will buckle you. The enemy will use your insecurities against you. This sensitive balance hinges on you surrendering to God and accepting that you are not perfect. This is not an excuse for sin but to remember you are victorious even after your mistakes.

Jesus set the greatest example of leadership:

1. He led as a servant while putting others' needs before His own. This is known as a Servant Leader. He demonstrated this when He washed the feet of His disciples in John 13:1–17.

2. He saw the good in others and did not condemn them. Christ inspired people to be their best selves. This style of leadership is a Charismatic Leader. He poured out His life so others would succeed. He loved unconditionally, even those who betrayed Him, decreasing that others would increase. Finally Jesus surrendered Himself to death that we

would have the gift of everlasting love.

3. Jesus projected and lived out the vision of obeying His heavenly Father and bringing the Kingdom of God to Earth. He was a team builder of His disciples and a relationship builder. This leadership style is called a Transformational Leader. He took time to know people, even people unlike Himself, by showing them love and compassion.

What kind of leader are you? What do you do to maintain a healthy outlook on your leadership role? Here are a few pointers:

- Take a time of respite to refuel.
- Be a continual student, sharpening your natural and spiritual skills.
- Surround yourself with people who believe in your vision and will encourage you to move forward. Align yourself with mentors who can pour experience and wisdom into your life.
- Continue to remind yourself why you said, "Yes," to your calling; rehearsing the impact you make in others' lives will refresh you every time.

Here is a quote to encourage you from "The 100 Best Leadership Quotes of All Time" (by Lolly Daskal):

"Leadership is not about titles, positions or flowcharts.

It is about one life influencing another."

John Maxwell – Pastor, Author and Speaker

As you walk in your divine purpose you will impact the lives that are connected to you. You will reach people no one else can reach. It's okay to take time to encourage yourself and remind yourself of who you are. Right now, God desires to use your life in the earth to empower someone, to help someone, or to be an extension of His hand and His heart. I Corinthians 15:58 shares, *"Therefore, my beloved brethren, be steadfast, immovable, always abounding in the work of the Lord, knowing that your labor is not in vain in the Lord."*

My friend, you are special in the eyes of God! You are awesome! You are strong! Great things are before you. Know that what God has bestowed upon you will be fulfilled! Each day, as you become more like Christ, your heart is accepting that the impossibilities are actually realities! It's time to go forward into the world strengthened, revived and refreshed to accomplish God's perfect plan!

"I will offer You my grateful heart, for I am Your unique creation, filled with wonder and awe!"

(Psalm 139:14, The Voice)

Conclusion

Thank you for sharing these refreshing moments with me. Be grateful that God gives you renewed moments; moments that restore you for the present day and future ones. Although life will bring its challenges, you have the confidence that your times are in God's hands. You have the confidence to know there is always a place of refreshing. You have the confidence to know that you are never alone. God has graced you to live during this generation and to make an eternal impact in the earth. You were created for such a time as this! You were meant to be born in these last days. You are a God-awakening moment, sent to Earth for this moment in history!

Fulfilling your purpose in your career, in ministry or in your personal life requires time, energy and strength. Please don't forgo utilizing your tools for refreshing for your soul, spirit and body need rest and rejuvenation on a regular basis. I connect my faith with yours. I believe you have grown through this reading experience and that the Kingdom of God has expanded. I believe that you will be better prepared to fulfill your purpose and be an asset to all connected to you.

Proverbs 11:25 (New Living Translation) summaries this book well: "*The generous will prosper; those who refresh others will themselves be refreshed.*" Now that you have read this book, you are in a position to share your restored strength with others so they too can be refreshed.

Gina

Time of Application

My father was a college professor after retiring from the Air Force. When I graduated from college with my undergrad degree, I had the privilege of teaching at Crafton Hills College in Southern California. My father shared with me three things about teaching effectively at a college level. He said these steps would ensure that the students had learned what they needed from class:

1. Teach the new concept
2. Give an example of the concept
3. Share how to apply that concept to daily living

Adult learners comprehend information in a greater capacity when they are able to apply concepts through real-life experiences. Here are some suggestions to assist you in getting the most understanding and revelation from this book. Life is more refreshing when you:

- Rehearse Affirmations:

- If I can see it, I can achieve it!
  - Every day is a new beginning!
  - I will fulfill my purpose in the earth!
  - I am a blessing to my family
- Recognize and journal God-awakening moments.
- Write out daily Thanksgiving. Try it for 30 days.
- Do something new or visit a new place.
- Practice random acts of kindness.
- Impart Eternity. Share with someone an eternal moment.
- Exercise "20 Refreshing Moments" that can impact your day positively. How refreshing:
  - To wake up with a grateful heart.
  - To see the manifestation of God's goodness around you.
  - To laugh and share joyful moments unexpectedly.
  - To be a part of corporate worship.
  - To gaze upon the beauty and breathtaking creation of God.
  - To have a chance to start all over again.
  - To love and be loved!
  - To give unto others by sowing a seed of kindness.
  - To observe "God-awakening" moments (miracles).

- To have spiritual and physical life!
- To remember the love and laughter of our family and friends whose address is now "Heaven".
- To read a scripture with a new revelation.
- To spend time with family, reminiscing about the good old days.
- To feel liberated to act silly sometimes with no apologies.
- To give honor to someone to whom honor is due.
- To eat a Girl Scout cookie that you've been waiting for all year, maybe even two.
- To laugh out loud until you cry.
- To see someone's life change for the better.
- To take a nap on Sunday afternoon without a care in the world.

Apply and enjoy these suggestions as you walk with a new refreshing outlook!

Other Books by Gina C. Edwards

- Imparting Eternity, 2014, published by Vision Directives
- Unearthing the Royalty from Within, 2017, Published by CreateSpace

To order please visit:
www.ginacedwards.com or www.Amazon.com

Biography

Gina C. Edwards, MSM, SHRM-CP is the founder of I Am Royalty Ministries and currently serves as a minister at Word Alive Worship Center (New Castle, DE), under the leadership of Pastors Anthony and Glenda Bailey. She is an author, speaker, worship leader, songwriter, and playwright. Gina has released two inspirational books; in 2017, *Unearthing the Royalty from Within* was published by Create Space and in 2014 she released *Imparting Eternity*, published by Vision Directives. She has worked in the human capital management field her entire career.

Gina enjoys encouraging others to fulfill their purpose through books, songs, plays, or speaking opportunities. She has spoken at the New Castle County Chamber Women's Expo, ACE Women's Network, Daughters of Esther and Women of Destiny Conferences as well as speaking frequently at her church. Gina enjoys spending time with her family and grandson Caleb, reading, traveling, going out to dinner and watching movies.

Gina has served on various community boards including DE SHRM (as president), the United Way HR Advisory Board and the Wilmington University HR Advisory Board. Gina also enjoys giving back to the community. She was an Adult Black Achiever alumnus through the YMCA and served as a mentor through the United Way "Women in Action" Leadership Program. Gina received her Bachelor of Arts Degree in business administration/MIS from California State University and is a 2017 honors graduate of Wilmington University with an MSM Degree in organizational leadership.

www.ingramcontent.com/pod-product-compliance
Lightning Source LLC
Chambersburg PA
CBHW071149090426
42736CB00012B/2283